SELECTED BY **JANE YOLEN**

SKY SCRAPE/CITY SCAPE

POEMS OF CITY LIFE

ILLUSTRATIONS BY **KEN CONDON**

Wordsong / Boyds Mills Press

Contents

City

In the morning the city
Spreads its wings
Making a song
In stone that sings.

In the evening the city
Goes to bed
Hanging lights
About its head.

Langston Hughes

Zebra

white sun
black
fire escape,

morning
grazing like a zebra
outside my window.

Judith Thurman

Sky Scrape/City Scape

Sky scrape,
City scape,
High stone,
Steel bone,
Cloud crown,
Smog gown,

Hurry up,
Hurry down.

Jane Yolen

Skyscraper

Skyscraper, skyscraper,
Scrape me some sky:
Tickle the sun
While the stars go by.

Tickle the stars
While the sun's climbing high,
Then skyscraper, skyscraper
Scrape me some sky.

Dennis Lee

Skyscrapers

Do skyscrapers ever grow tired
Of holding themselves up high?
Do they ever shiver on frosty nights
With their tops against the sky?
Do they feel lonely sometimes
Because they have grown so tall?
Do they ever wish they could lie right down
And never get up at all?

Rachel Field

Prayers of Steel

Lay me on an anvil, O God.
Beat me and hammer me into a crowbar.
Let me pry loose old walls.
Let me lift and loosen old foundations.

Lay me on an anvil, O God.
Beat me and hammer me into a steel spike.
Drive me into the girders that hold a skyscraper together.
Take red-hot rivets and fasten me into the central girders.
Let me be the great nail holding a skyscraper through blue nights into
        white stars.

Carl Sandburg

A Lazy Thought

There go the grownups
To the office,
To the store.
Subway rush,
Traffic crush;
Hurry, scurry,
Worry, flurry.

No wonder
Grownups
Don't grow up
Any more.

It takes a lot
Of slow
To grow.

Eve Merriam

The Subway Train

The subway train, the
    subway train,
If you'll permit me to explain,
Is like a busy beetle black
That scoots along a silver track;
And, whether it be night or day,
The beetle has to light its way,
Because the only place it's
    found
Is deep, deep, deep, deep, under-
    ground.

Leland B. Jacobs

Commuters

Like the city skyline they
continue day after day,
bone to dust, stone to sand,
steel to rust, choices
to swaying from straps.

Betsy Hearne

Red-Dress Girl

The rope swings in
and out, sister dances
over the rope
her red dress flying,
and the feet in the sneakers go
spank-dab, spank-dab.

I got dizzy watching
she's so smooth
more like *she* stood still
and the rope flew round
her.

Mother called, "Come in."
She never minded,
her face calm
as an old moon
that red dress
flying.

Ann Turner

74th Street

Hey, this little kid gets roller skates.
She puts them on.
She stands up and almost
flops over backwards.
She sticks out a foot like
she's going somewhere and
falls down and
smacks her hand. She
grabs hold of a step to get up and
sticks out the other foot and
slides about six inches and
falls and
skins her knee.

And then, you know what?

She brushes off the dirt and the
blood and puts some
spit on it and then
sticks out the other foot

again.

Myra Cohn Livingston

Pigeons

Pigeons are city folk
content
to live with concrete
and cement.

They seldom
try
the sky.

A pigeon never sings
of hill
and flowering hedge,
but busily commutes
from sidewalk
to his ledge.

Oh pigeon, what a waste of wings!

Lilian Moore

Red Flower

I went by this building,
brown, mostly gray
like all the city smoke
and noise got ground
into those bricks,
the window glass so black
it looked like tar.

And I thought, Nobody
lives there—too quiet,
too dark, too gray,
when I looked up and saw
one window open,
the curtains blowing in
and a red flower blooming.

Ann Turner

Graffiti

I read a sad poem
on the wall
on my way to school:

*Some Day Sugar
You Gonna Find
No One In The World
Gonna Give You Sweet*

But I thought of Mama
ironing my skirt
this morning,
Daddy giving me
a brand new box of crayons,
and all my aunts and uncles
lining up for hugs
yesterday,
a whole day
before my birthday.

Sweet may not be
a box of candy;
sweet may not be
a chocolate birthday cake.
But you can taste it
your whole life long.

Anyway—
what does someone know
who has to use a wall
to write a poem?

Jane Yolen

A Rumble

They roar
Out of the river tunnels
Into the streaming streets,
As strong
As a pride of lions,
As long
As a gaggle of geese.
A rumble of trucks
Streaks through the city.
I'd like to drive one
Towering over taxis,
Diesels smoking!
I'd like to drive one,
Cars pulling over,
Cops waving!
I'd like to streak
Through the city
Part of
A rumble of trucks.

Virginia Schonborg

Oil Slick

There, by the curb,
a leaky truck
has drooled
a grease-pool,

a black, pearly
slick
which rainbows
when the sun
strikes it.

I could spend
all day
marbling
its flashy colors
with a stick.

Judith Thurman

Flash

Signs on 42nd Street
flash—
blue, green, red, yellow,
looking like fireworks
fighting hard
to explode.

Lee Bennett Hopkins

18

J's the Jumping Jay-Walker

J's the jumping Jay-walker,
 A sort of human jeep.
He crosses where the lights are red.
 Before he looks, he'll leap!
Then many a wheel
Begins to squeal,
 And many a brake to slam.
He turns your knees to jelly
 And the traffic into jam.

Phyllis McGinley

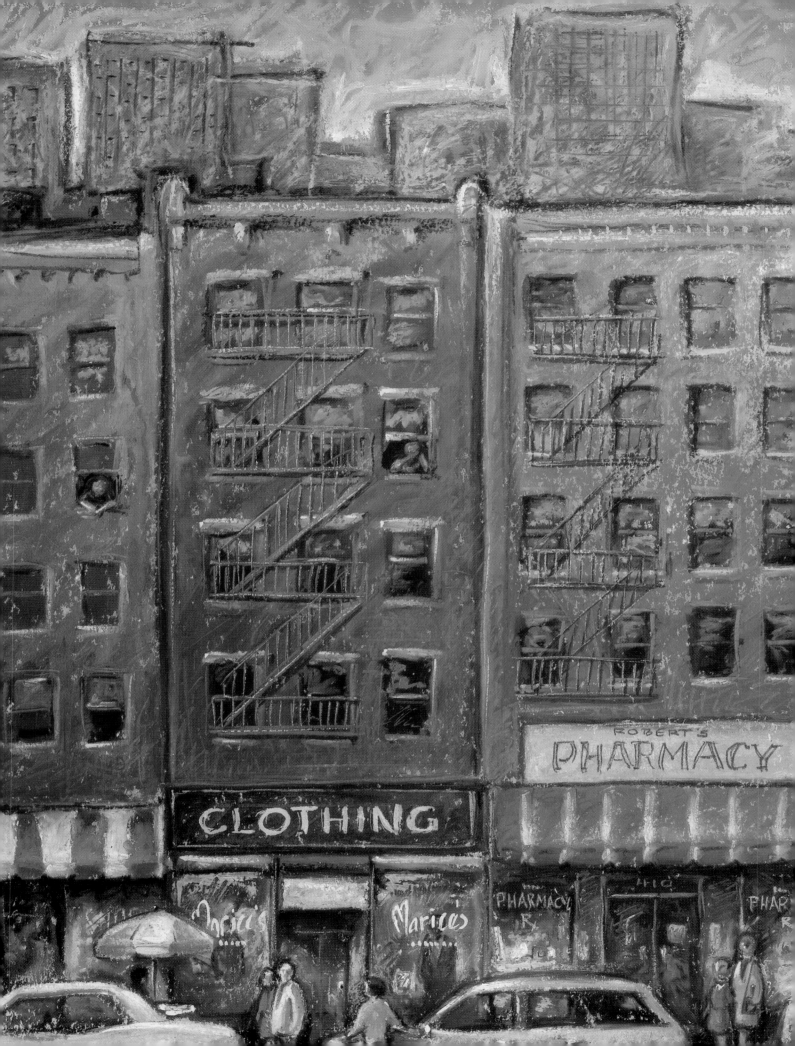

In the Inner City

in the inner city
or
like we call it
home
we think a lot about uptown
and the silent nights
and the houses straight as
dead men
and the pastel lights
and we hang on to our no place
happy to be alive
and in the inner city
or
like we call it
home

Lucille Clifton

Envoi: Washington Square Park

(For Margaret K. McElderry)

Wind in the park
and the children swing
in the world of the green

in the wind on the leaves
and the children shout
in the wind in the park

and the joggers sprint
and the small birds sing
in the world of the green

and the dogs run free
and birds fly about
in the wind in the park

and the children go
and the light fades out
in the wind in the park
in the world of the green

Myra Cohn Livingston

City Park

In the shade of a plane tree with our shopping
We watch the marvelous clouds glide over.
The city round us hums like bees
And buses dart like dragonflies
Between the reedbeds of the trees.
It is half past five of a hot afternoon,
And the little old woman
Who lives alone without a garden
Will soon appear with her bag of crumbs
To feed the water birds on the lake by the fountain.
"The ducks are dirty," she chirps like a sparrow,
"But the swans are clean, so very clean.
I could lie on their backs like a lovely armchair
And fly away almost anywhere."

Christine Crow

The Streetcleaner's Lament

dirt and
clean them clean them clean them
dirt and
leave them let them rot
dirt and stench and
clean them clean them
bending at the waist and stabbing—
papers papers blowing sticking
never leave them
clean them clean them
people put them
now remove them
clean streets sidewalks
quick
remove them
dirt and dirt and dirt forever.

Patricia Hubbell

Clean

When I was small
like five,
lived in a place
where they washed the streets.
I'd hear them at four
outside my window,
wheels rumble silent,
the swish of big brushes,
the hosing down—like steam.
And I'd think (but too
sleepy to do!)
about going out
and bouncing a red ball
down those streets,
just me—and the ball
on those clean,
sweet streets.

Ann Turner

The City Dump

City asleep
City asleep
Papers fly at the garbage heap.
Refuse dumped and
The sea gulls reap
Grapefruit rinds
And coffee grinds
And apple peels.
The sea gull reels and
The field mouse steals
In for a bite
At the end of night
Of crusts and crumbs
And pits of plums.
The white eggshells
And the blue-green smells
And the gray gull's cry
And the red dawn sky . . .
City asleep
City asleep
A carnival
On the garbage heap.

Felice Holman

Manhattan Lullaby

Lulled by rumble, babble, beep,
let these little children sleep;
let these city girls and boys
dream a music in the noise,
hear a tune their city plucks
up from buses, up from trucks
up from engines wailing *fire!*
up ten stories high, and higher,
up from hammers, rivets, drills,
up tall buildings, over sills,
up where city children sleep,
lulled by rumble, babble, beep.

Norma Farber

To **Brandon Piatt**, a country boy in the big city — J.Y.

To **Jeannine** and **Caroline** — K.C.

Published by Wordsong
Boyds Mills Press, Inc.
A Highlights Company
815 Church Street
Honesdale, Pennsylvania 18431
Printed in Mexico

Publisher Cataloging-in-Publication Data
Sky scrape/city scape : poems of city life / selected by Jane
Yolen ; illustrations by Ken Condon.—1st ed.
[32]p. : col. ill. ; cm.
Summary : An anthology of poems by Langston Hughes, Jane
Yolen, Rachel Field, and others depicts the sights, sounds, and
energy of the city.
ISBN 1-56397-179-8
1. City and town life—Juvenile Poetry. 2. Children's Poetry—
Collections. [1. City and town life—Poetry. 2. Poetry—
Collections.] I. Yolen, Jane. II. Condon, Ken, ill. III. Title.
808.81—dc20   1996   AC
Library of Congress Catalog Card Number 92-61940

First edition, 1996
Book designed by Joy Chu
The text of this book is set in 18-point Times Roman.
The illustrations are done in chalk and oil pastel.
Distributed by St. Martin's Press

10 9 8 7 6 5 4 3 2 1

Acknowledgments

*Every possible effort has been made to trace the ownership of each poem
included in SKY SCRAPE / CITY SCAPE. If any errors or omissions have
occurred, corrections will be made in subsequent printings, provided the
publisher is notified of their existence.*

*Permission to reprint copyrighted poems is gratefully acknowledged to the
following:*

*Alfred A. Knopf, Inc., for "City" from COLLECTED POEMS by Langston
Hughes. Copyright © 1994 by the Estate of Langston Hughes. Reprinted by
permission of Alfred A. Knopf, Inc.*

*Atheneum for "Skyscrapers" from POEMS by Rachel Field (New York:
Macmillan, 1957); and "The Streetcleaner's Lament" from 8 A.M. SHADOWS by
Patricia Hubbell. Copyright © 1965, and renewed © 1993, by Patricia
Hubbell. Reprinted by permission of Atheneum Books for Young Readers, an
imprint of Simon & Schuster Children's Publishing Division.*

*BOA Editions, Ltd., for "in the inner city," copyright © 1987 by Lucille Clifton.
Reprinted from GOOD WOMAN: POEMS AND A MEMOIR 1969-1980 by Lucille
Clifton, with permission of BOA Editions, Ltd., 92 Park Ave., Brockport, NY
14420.*

Christine Crow for "City Park." Copyright © 1996 by Christine Crow.

*Curtis Brown, Ltd., for "J's the Jumping Jay-Walker" from ALL AROUND TOWN
by Phyllis McGinley. Originally published by J.B. Lippincott Co. Copyright
© 1948 by Phyllis McGinley; "Graffiti" and "Sky Scrape / City Scape" by Jane
Yolen. Copyright © 1996 by Jane Yolen; and "Flash" from PASS THE POETRY,
PLEASE! by Lee Bennett Hopkins. Originally published by Harper & Row.
Copyright © 1972 by Lee Bennett Hopkins.*

*Thomas Farber for "Manhattan Lullaby" by Norma Farber. Copyright by
Thomas Farber.*

*Harcourt Brace & Co. for "Prayers of Steel" from CORNHUSKERS by Carl
Sandburg. Copyright © 1918 by Harcourt Brace Jovanovich, Inc., and
renewed 1946 by Carl Sandburg. Reprinted by permission of the publisher.*

*Henry Holt and Company, Inc., for "The Subway Train" from IS SOMEWHERE
ALWAYS FAR AWAY? by Leland B. Jacobs. Copyright © 1967 by Leland B.
Jacobs. Reprinted by permission of Henry Holt and Company, Inc.*

*Houghton Mifflin Co. for "Red Flower," "Clean," and "Red-Dress Girl" from
STREET TALK by Ann Turner. Copyright © 1986 by Ann Turner. Reprinted by
permission of Houghton Mifflin Co. All rights reserved.*

*Margaret K. McElderry Books for "Commuters" from POLAROID AND OTHER
POEMS OF VIEW by Betsy Hearne. Copyright © 1991 by Betsy Hearne; and
"Envoi: Washington Square Park" from REMEMBERING AND OTHER POEMS by
Myra Cohn Livingston. Copyright © 1989 by Myra Cohn Livingston.
Reprinted by permission of Margaret K. McElderry Books, an imprint of Simon
& Schuster Children's Publishing Division.*

*MGA Agency, Inc., for "Skyscraper" by Dennis Lee. Copyright © 1974 by
Dennis Lee. Reprinted by permission of MGA Agency, Inc.*

*Marian Reiner for "74th Street" from THE MALIBU AND OTHER POEMS by
Myra Cohn Livingston. Copyright © 1972 by Myra Cohn Livingston; "A Lazy
Thought" from JAMBOREE RHYMES FOR ALL TIMES by Eve Merriam.
Copyright © 1962, 1964, 1966, 1973, 1984 by Eve Merriam; "Pigeons" from
I THOUGHT I HEARD THE CITY by Lilian Moore. Copyright © 1969 by Lilian
Moore; and "Zebra" and "Oil Slick" from FLASHLIGHT AND OTHER POEMS by
Judith Thurman. Copyright © 1976 by Judith Thurman. Reprinted by
permission of Marian Reiner for the authors.*

*William Morrow and Company, Inc., for "A Rumble" from SUBWAY SWINGER by
Virginia Schonborg. Copyright © 1970 by Virginia Schonborg. Reprinted by
permission of Morrow Junior Books, a division of William Morrow and
Company, Inc.*